Cocurricular Activities:
Their Values and Benefits

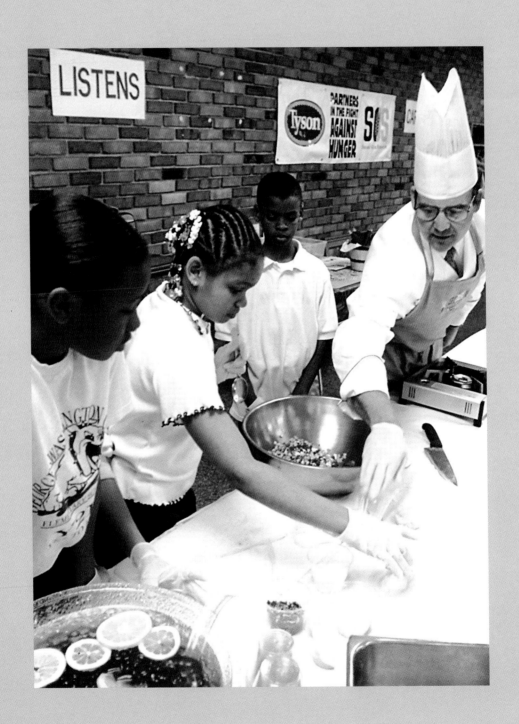

Cocurricular Activities:
Their Values and Benefits

Community Service
Lending a Hand

Terry Callahan

Mason Crest Publishers
Philadelphia

Mason Crest Publishers, Inc.
370 Reed Road
Broomall, PA 19008
(866) MCP-BOOK (toll free)
www.masoncrest.com

First printing

1 2 3 4 5 6 7 8 9 10

Library of Congress Cataloging-in-Publication Data

Callahan, Terry.
  Community service: lending a hand/by Terry Callahan.
      p. cm.—(Cocurricular activities)
  Includes index.
  ISBN 1-59084-891-8
  1. Student service. I. Title. II. Series.
  LC220.5.C355 2005

      2004015856

Produced by
Choptank Syndicate, Inc. and Chestnut Productions, L.L.C.
260 Upper Moss Hill Road
Russell, Massachusetts 01071

Project Editors Norman Macht and Mary Hull
Design and Production Lisa Hochstein
Picture Research Mary Hull

OPPOSITE TITLE PAGE

Students from George Washington Carver Elementary School help prepare low-cost dishes for Share Our Strength's Operation Frontline, a national nutritional education program for at-risk individuals.

Table of Contents

Introduction

COCURRICULAR ACTIVITIES BUILD CHARACTER

Sharon L. Ransom
Chief Officer of the Office of Standards-Based Instruction
for Chicago Public Schools

Cocurricular activities provide an assortment of athletic, musical, cultural, dramatic, club, and service activities. They provide opportunities based on different talents and interests for students to find their niche while developing character. Character is who we really are. It's what we say and how we say it, what we think, what we value, and how we conduct ourselves in difficult situations. It is character that often determines our success in life and cocurricular activities play a significant role in the development of character in young men and women.

Cocurricular programs and activities provide opportunities to channel the interests and talents of students into positive efforts for the betterment of themselves and the community as a whole. Students who participate in cocurricular activities are often expected to follow certain rules and regulations that prepare them for challenges as well as opportunities later in life.

Many qualities that build character are often taught and nurtured through participation in cocurricular activities. A student learns to make commitments and stick with them through victories and losses as well as achievements and disappointments. They can also learn to build relationships and work collaboratively with others, set goals, and follow the principles and rules of the discipline, club, activity, or sport in which they participate.

Students who are active in cocurricular activities are often successful in school because the traits and behaviors they learn outside of the classroom are important in acquiring and maintaining their academic success. Students become committed to their studies and set academic goals that lead them to triumph. When they relate behaviors, such as following rules or directions or teaming with others, to the classroom, this can result in improved academic achievement.

Students who participate in cocurricular activities and acquire these character-rich behaviors and traits are not likely to be involved in negative behaviors. Peer pressure and negative influences are not as strong for these students, and they are not likely to be involved with drugs, alcohol, or tobacco use. They also attend school more regularly and are less likely to drop out of school.

Students involved in cocurricular activities often are coached or mentored by successful and ethical adults of good and strong character who serve as role models and assist students in setting their goals for the future. These students are also more likely to graduate from high school and go on to college because of their involvement in co-curricular activities.

In this series you will come to realize the many benefits of cocurricular activities. These activities bring success and benefits to individual students, the school, and the community.

By participating in community service activities, students help their community and they learn leadership and social skills that prepare them for the future.

Teens Taking Charge

Imagine many groups of middle and high school students sitting down to discuss the results of their research—results that include helping to decide how to spend millions of dollars.

That is what happens in Michigan's Youth Advisory Councils (YAC). Almost fifteen hundred youths act as grantmakers who work to determine the needs of their communities. They review grant applications to see if the proposed project will help meet community needs. They interview people who are applying for the grants to get more information. Some members may go out and check prices to see if the prices for grant items are accurate. When all their research and studies have been completed, the students meet and discuss their findings with their adult advisor. If they are satisfied with the information and the potential effectiveness of the grant, they tell the adult board members that they support the grant proposal and recommend the money be released.

A Youth Advisory Grant to the Rocky Mountain Youth Corps funded the construction of this "free expression" wall at a skateboard park in Taos, New Mexico.

Although it is the adult board members who make the final grant decisions, generally they follow the students' recommendations. At stake is nearly $48 million in permanently endowed youth funds from the W. K. Kellogg Foundation, money that is matched with more than $100 million generated locally. "To apply knowledge to solve the problems of people" is the mission of the W. K. Kellogg Foundation, which began the initiative, "Learning In Deed: Making a Difference Through Service Learning" in 1998.

The responsibilities of the YAC student grantmakers do not end there. After the grants are made, the students act as observers to make sure the grants are being carried out as planned. In addition, because the effects of their efforts have been so beneficial to the communities, many nonprofit organizations ask to have YAC members on their boards, too.

A recent YAC "Great Grants" finalist received funds for a "graffiti wall" so community members could express themselves in words and pictures. The project resulted in greater community involvement in civic issues. Reading Buddies funds were used to purchase books to tutor at-risk elementary students and support a teen center that includes study areas, minimal-cost programs, and tutoring during exam time. The YAC Web site posts additional grant recipients, including a program in which homeless children help at an animal shelter, and a multicultural drum and dance organization.

Students are having huge impacts on their communities.

Humane Teen of the Year

The Humane Society of the United States selected Ariel Kravitz as their 2003 Humane Teen of the Year. A volunteer at the North Shore Animal League in New York, she took animals out of their cages and played with them to retain or increase their socialization skills with humans. She observed their unique personalities and tried to get the animals matched with a family that was appropriate for them, then made post-adoption calls to make sure the pet had settled into its new home.

Kravitz also worked with students in a therapeutic riding program as a "lead walker," controlling the behavior of the horse ridden by a rider with special needs. After seeing the progress made in posture and interest by these riders, she said, "I believe that the volunteers in such programs benefit the most. There is no better feeling than turning a passion into something meaningful." On its Web site **<www.humaneteen.org>** the Humane Society of the United States has profiles of additional teens and young adults who have taken time to help animals in need.

Some call what they are doing community service; others call it service-learning. While Maryland became the only state to add service-learning as a statewide public school graduation requirement beginning in 1993, today schools in all fifty states offer service-learning. Not only do students make connections, they find that their actions can have far-reaching effects.

Sometimes students perform service projects through school classes or organizations. Sometimes they work with

Yoshiyama Awards

Many businesses from other countries have branches in the United States, and many U.S. companies have branches abroad. Some companies feel that it is important to establish a partnership with the countries in which they are based.

The Hitachi Foundation **<www.hitachi.org>** was established to improve the quality of life for underserved people in the U.S. and to help Hitachi, a Japanese-based organization, "learn how to better fulfill its responsibilities as a corporate citizen doing business in the United States."

According to Hirokichi Yoshiyama, Chairman Emeritus of Hitachi, Ltd., "Each of us must take the initiative in addressing society's problems as if they were our own individual concerns. If we do, we can surmount today's difficulties and create a brighter world for people everywhere." The $5,000 awards that bear his name are given annually to ten U.S. high school seniors on the basis of their community service activities.

Recent finalists include the founder of a pediatric cancer fund; a student who founded Suitcases for Kids to provide foster children with their own luggage; a student who got the school athletic policy changed to eliminate gender-based differences; and a student who founded an outreach program to help students with mental illnesses.

National Youth of the Year winner Raymond Nunez, second from right, poses with Boys and Girls Club member Mark Wahlberg and the 2001 regional winners in front of the White House.

religion-based or other community groups, such as the Lions, the Elks, the Rotary, or the Moose. And sometimes they see a need and are motivated to do something about it as concerned individuals. For example, Annie Wignall of Iowa began the Care Bags Foundation when she was eleven years old. This organization collects and distributes clothes, toys, and personal care items for children who are victims of abuse or neglect. As a result, she was recognized by President George W. Bush for her efforts. Other out-standing youth have been recognized through Presidential Freedom Scholarships and the President's Volunteer Service Awards.

A recent National Youth of the Year winner, Raymond Nunez of the Lawrence, Massachusetts, Boys and Girls

Inspired by the plight of homeless pets, Brigid Cleary, left, and Angela Cortiz, affiliated with the Web site agirlsworld.com, collaborated with the North County Humane Society to create a Web-based game that encourages families to spay their cats and dogs.

Club, was recognized for his service to his peers and his community in tutoring, neighborhood cleanup efforts, buying books for underprivileged children at Christmas, and as president of the TEENSupreme® Keystone Club. A recent regional finalist for this award, Melissa Vigil of New Mexico, volunteered in programs to feed the hungry and started teen literacy programs.

Lauren and Meghan Galvin and Ashle Worrick were recognized in *USA Weekend* for their Make a Difference Day project: raising money to send young cancer patients to a camp especially geared to their needs. They collected autographed celebrity hats and clothing to model and auction, raising $9,000, nine times their goal.

By helping children with special needs, serving in a soup kitchen, tutoring or mentoring their peers, restoring a community park, or participating in countless other service projects, students fill important roles in the wellbeing of their communities.

Leukemia ambassador Adam Lopez and Mandy Moore, the honorary chairperson of the Leukemia and Lymphoma Society's School and Youth Programs, recently presented the society with a check for $2.2 million raised by schoolchildren.

2

Serving for Safety and Health

Two issues important to everyone are maintaining a safe community and promoting the health of community members. Cocurricular service projects can help accomplish these goals.

Ways to address safety issues with those who need the advice most include presentations and projects that give children the means to make wise decisions. In Clearfield, Utah, children attended a bicycle safety camp sponsored by several community groups. The children participated in several community-run safety "stations," received new bike helmets, and got to ride a rodeo course. This event was held during Join Hands Day, a national event that links young people and adults to make their communities better.

A Family, Career, and Community Leaders of America (FCCLA) member from Monroe Central Jr./Sr. High School in Indiana addressed bike safety in a FCCLA chapter project. She showed second graders what important safety features to look for when choosing a new bike.

Each year, the DECA (an association of marketing students) chapter at Ridgewood High School in Illinois works with local police and fire departments, the local mall, and the school's marketing department to run Safety Town. This program helps students learn to cross streets safely. Staffed by student volunteers, the Safety Town program also includes explanations of car safety, seatbelt use, and fire safety.

Student Council members at North Community High School in Minnesota have targeted seatbelt safety. They stand in the student parking lot each morning for a week in February or March and check to see that the drivers and passengers are wearing their seatbelts. Besides hanging posters of mangled cars and presenting awareness activities, they also compile their statistics for the week to be used as part of a safety conference report.

Used cell phones can be collected and donated to a service that reprograms them to automatically dial 911. The cell phones are then donated to the elderly and others in need in the community, such as victims of domestic violence, to provide them the means of summoning help should they need it. The cell phone drive held by the National Honor Society chapter at West High School in Manchester, New Hampshire, was so successful that they were able to donate nearly two hundred cell phones to the project.

The Technology Student Association (TSA) promotes Internet safety through a program called I-Safe America. Its goal is "to combat widespread victimization of young people on the Internet" by giving youths "the critical thinking and decision-making skills they need to be safe online," says Teri Schroeder, founder and CEO of I-Safe.

Other safety projects nationwide include talks by FCCLA

Each year on Join Hands Day, students participate in community service projects that include picking up trash, planting flowers and shrubs, removing graffiti, collecting toys, books, and clothes for needy children, and helping the elderly with home maintenance.

members in North Dakota's Velva Public Schools covering a wide variety of safety topics such as sun safety and precautions, chemical safety, and proper 911 use. DECA members in Suffolk, Virginia, work with elementary children to promote dog safety so the young students will not get bitten. The presentation includes several videotapes, informational packets for the children and their families, and guest speakers from the community. Some student groups nationwide perform skits or puppet shows on being careful around strangers and dealing with bullies.

Projects such as these are examples of peer mentoring. Peer mentoring involves a student helping another person to learn new material or to reinforce previously-learned skills. One type of mentoring is one-on-one peer listening. A good strategy is to choose core listeners from a variety of "image" groups within the school. These listeners are then trained in communications skills and in making referrals of specific issues to the correct resource person or group.

Peer mediation, also called conflict mediation or conflict resolution, is available in over 50 percent of U.S. schools. Often, peer mediators are nominated by their peers and chosen from all image groups in the school.

Students are trained from middle level grades through high school, depending on a school's or district's program, to work with students who are having problems with other students. Peer mediators may work with the students who are experiencing the conflict as part of a class, with a counselor, or as peer mediation partners. Peer mediators at John Marshall Middle School in California were trained in cultural diversity, tolerance, and conflict resolution. They then presented workshops and an assembly on school violence in partnership with the Long Beach Police Department's Gang Unit. These activities help bring students of different backgrounds together to communicate about related problems and discuss how to resolve these situations.

There are guidelines to mediations. For example, the students experiencing the difficulty might first be asked to write down their versions of the problem. The students are then told the rules they must follow during the mediation. These rules include no interrupting, no put-downs, and no discussion of the mediation conversation afterwards by any of the persons present, including the mediators, to insure confidentiality.

Peer mediators are trained to be non-judgmental. They

will listen to each side of the story, one person at a time, restate what they understand the issues to be, and help the students try to come up with a solution to their problem. Students must agree to the solution. If they cannot come to agreement, the situation will then be referred to a counselor or administrator.

Protection for Police Dogs

Emily Bolton, a student at Smithburg Middle School in Maryland, was inspired to develop her "Vest-A-Dog" program after she read a story about a police dog that had been shot in the line of duty, causing a California student to raise money for bullet-proof vests for police dogs. Bolton's goal was to raise enough money to buy vests for the dogs in her city, sheriff's, and local state police branches. Vests cost $500 each, so her initial goal was to raise enough to outfit ten dogs.

Through newspaper articles, donation containers in businesses, group presentations, and letter writing, she was able to raise over $13,000 to purchase 26 vests and 20 pairs of protective booties. As recognition for her efforts, Bolton was named both an honorary Washington County Sheriff's Deputy and an honorary Maryland State Trooper.

Bolton plans to become a veterinarian and says, "I encourage and challenge other students to do similar projects." In doing so, she feels that young people will see that they can make a difference in their communities.

A Florida student, Stacey Hillman, was awarded a Prudential Spirit of Community Award for her efforts to protect police dogs. Several years ago she started Pennies to Protect Police Dogs, a project that has since raised over $200,000. Hillman's award was $25,000 worth of clothing and toys to be donated to a charity of her choice. She donated her prize to the Volusia and Osceola Sheriff's offices.

Peer mediation is an effective way to prevent students from receiving discipline referrals while helping them learn to work out their issues. Peer mediators may be supervised by the sponsor of an organization such as the Student Government Association or the National Honor Society, by a counselor or administrator, or by any teacher who has shown interest in the process and received the training.

There is also peer-education, in which a small group of older teens works with a larger group of younger students to communicate a prevention or service message, then join the younger students in a related service project.

FCCLA members participate in a program called STOP the Violence: Students Taking On Prevention. This program's goals are to "recognize, report, and reduce youth violence." Member volunteers are given training to enable them to recognize warning signs of youth violence, including bullying. They also educate their peers about violence prevention and encourage them to report behavior that might signal potential danger. These trained peer educators work with their school and community on issues of youth violence. Students in grades six through nine learn the basic issues of youth violence, while older students learn more in-depth information and are taught how to develop projects to address these concerns.

Examples of FCCLA chapter projects include holding a Halloween party with non-violent customs, decorating a holiday tree with the names of students who have pledged to reject violence, and holding a candlelight ceremony at an assembly. John P. Stevens High School in Edison, New Jersey, only thirty miles from New York City, developed a STOP the Violence project to help unite its multicultural community.

Another peer program is Teen Court. The Brown County,

South Dakota, Teen Court is a volunteer program that helps teenage offenders assume responsibility for their behavior. "Offenders are brought before a jury of their peers where they are appropriately sentenced to fit the crime they have committed." Their mission statement also says that "we believe these individuals deserve to be treated with respect and dignity." Therefore, the court's involvement should be performed in a professional manner.

In Teen Court, students take over courtroom roles, from attorneys to judges to jurors, in helping decide what consequences their peers should receive for misconduct in the community. Teen volunteers must attend meetings, trainings, and the court sessions. Students who appear before Teen Court choose to do so and abide by their peers' decisions. They may also be required to participate in one or more Teen Court sessions to experience another point of view. By fulfilling their sentence requirements, first-time offenders can keep a clean record. Students who fail to comply face referral to other agencies.

In VIVA (Voices for Interpersonal Violence Alternatives), students act out relationship scenarios, usually dealing with unpleasant dating or harassment issues. After the performances, the teen actors from the Charlottesville and Albermarle, Virginia areas assist as the audience breaks into smaller groups, each with a trained facilitator, to discuss what they saw happening and what they want in their own interpersonal relationships.

At Florida's Loften High School the Hippodrome Improvisational Teen Theatre works with a variety of students in workshops that promote self-expression, communication, and conflict mediation skills. They perform at 26 area schools and program sites to a total audience of over 2,700 students.

An FCCLA member talks with a reporter about STOP the Violence—Students Taking on Prevention, a national FCCLA peer-to-peer outreach initiative that empowers young people to recognize, report, and reduce the potential for violence in their schools and communities.

Additional opportunities for students to prevent crime are available through school watch programs, safety patrols, and, in some communities, police explorer programs to learn about a career in law enforcement. Many law enforcement agencies have programs in which they give away stuffed toys to children. Student organizations can hold events to collect new bears or raise money for the agency to purchase them. These agencies sometimes hold open houses, bicycle safety programs, violent toy collections, and drug awareness programs in which teens can help.

When over one hundred cats, many malnourished and sick with feline HIV, were found in a residence in a neighboring county, students throughout Talbot County, Maryland decided to get involved. While some students independently collected supplies for the animals, who were placed in shelters in two counties, three sixth-grade classes at Easton Middle School held a penny drive to buy supplies for the animals. While only pennies were requested, many of the students donated any change they had. Some students also worked with local businesses to collect donations. Students donated money and needed items such as pet food, cat litter, newspaper for animal crates, toys, towels, and blankets. At the end of the activity, students had donated over $400 and two carts of supplies.

Safety issues arise from the use of illegal substances, and there are a number of service-based organizations that focus on this area. SHOP (Students Helping Other People) and Trendsetters are two active cocurricular programs dealing with substance abuse. In the middle grades, activities promote awareness. A group might design a display of advertisements and describe how they try to appeal to young people. A collection of such advertisements could be made, followed by a celebration as they are thrown out, symbolizing students' rejection of these products.

Both Trendsetters and SHOP can be conducted through classes such as health or physical education or as after-school activities. SHOP members promote awareness of substance abuse issues, advocate for changes in laws (banning smoking in public places, for example), create public service announcements, participate in fundraising activities such as Relay for Life or March of Dimes, hold assemblies, and promote a healthy lifestyle. Many substance awareness groups such as these participate in a variety of special days and events sponsored by the American Lung Association, the American Heart Association, and the American Cancer Society.

Gabriel Wilson, a senior at Ohio's Northland High School, was recognized by President George W. Bush for his active role in helping younger students reject drug use and peer pressure. Wilson has served on Youth to Youth's Youth Advisory and Speakers Boards, helping design and put into practice drug prevention programs and speaking to his peers about the benefits of making drug-free choices.

A national activity to promote a healthy, drug-free lifestyle is Red Ribbon Week, when organizations such as SHOP and FCCLA prepare activities to promote awareness of drug and alcohol use among students of all ages, including related coloring pages, word searches, or assemblies. The Red Ribbon is given out during the week to symbolize a pledge toward a drug-free lifestyle. Activities vary but may include a "wear red" day, a pledge-signing day, and a day to present ribbons to younger students.

Some schools and organizations connect Red Ribbon Week to other school programs such as Character Counts, an education framework that promotes the Six Pillars of Character: trustworthiness, respect, responsibility, fairness, caring, and citizenship. St. John the Baptist Parish Schools won Louisiana's 2003–2004 Red Ribbon Parish of the Year award through their efforts to teach character as a means of helping students avoid a lifestyle that leads to drugs. In Character Counts programs in many states, students are trained to act as peer mentors, going into classrooms and presenting related character topics to younger students.

The American Red Cross is a well-known organization that promotes collaborations between local Red Cross chapters and youth organizations to unite their strengths for the benefit of their communities. Examples of youth activities range from fundraising activities such as the car wash event "Wash America," organized by two sisters in Virginia to help families affected by the events of September 11, 2001, to the Delaware TSA's whipped cream pie throw, in which the proceeds were donated to the Red Cross. In the San Francisco Bay Red Cross chapter, students use peer education to involve middle and high school students in the fight against AIDS/HIV, while through the Greater Buffalo, New York, chapter, students help elderly community residents stay independent longer by performing light housekeeping, yard work, and pet care services.

UNICEF (United Nations Children's Fund) has long partnered with children at Halloween as they collected money to help children worldwide. However, UNICEF needs do not stop after Halloween. The organization meets medical, nutritional, health, and education needs year-round, along with emergency relief operations, such as helping children in Iran after a terrible earthquake destroyed much of their city. Groups or individuals can contact UNICEF to find fundraising and project ideas at any time.

Canadian Youth Program Helps the Community

The St. John Ambulance Cadets, started over 75 years ago, now can be found in over 60 countries. According to the Web site <www.sja-haltonhills.org>, "What sets the St. John Ambulance youth corps apart from any other is the first aid and health care training, and the chance to use and develop those skills in 'real life' while working at community events under the supervision of Adult Patient Care Providers." The Canadian program offers opportunities to Juniors (ages six to ten) at many sites. These activities focus on friends, sharing, safety, crafts, games, and helping others. Cadets, ages eleven to fifteen, focus on first aid, friends, confidence, and self-esteem as they attend trainings, competitions, and camp; develop skills; and help the first aid staff at community events. Crusaders, who are sixteen or older, are part of the first aid staff; attend patient care competitions; and receive advanced training.

Students from Hartford, Connecticut, organized a food collection to benefit their local food bank, which distributes provisions to community members.

Unfortunately, disasters can and do happen. Students at Massac County High School in Illinois launched Operation Tornado 2003 after a tornado destroyed local businesses, homes, and farms. Students not only divided into groups to handle area cleanup needs in an effort that took over 190 hours, they also collected over $900 in donations and held a scavenger hunt to collect care packages for affected families, gathering over 900 items. This project earned them recognition by the National Honor Society as one of the year's ten outstanding service projects in the nation.

Malcolm Shabazz City High School students in Madison, Wisconsin, have been cited on the Learning In Deed Web site for their projects involving local immigrants. Putting their classroom skills to work, they interviewed immigrants, researched the countries of their origin, and wrote letters to public officials "advocating for human rights and an end to the violence that threatens refugees."

Students also advocate for health issues, often as a result of experiences from an internship program. One student intern in the Philadelphia school district became an advocate of stress tests to diagnose coronary heart disease. She created pamphlets to go along with her presentations on the subject and requested that students spread the word to their family and friends. The clinic where she interned decided to give her pamphlet to their patients and visitors.

Another Learning In Deed project is the partnership between the Healthcare Science and Technology (HST) department at Phenix City Schools and Alabama dental and medical associations. Together they helped students learn preventative health care skills by presenting information on hand washing, oral hygiene, and diabetes. The HST students also held community blood sugar screenings.

In Oregon, Crook County High School students worked to inform the community of the importance of child vaccinations, organized a health fair, provided free blood pressure checks, updated the community on health issues, and held an assembly about trauma injuries related to the misuse of alcohol. Students at the Baltimore City Career Academy in Maryland held an event called "AIDS: A Day, A Difference." After researching the topic and area statistics, they developed the AIDS awareness and education event for students and community members that included informational games, dramatic skits, and other presentations.

Students can find many ways to work with their schools and communities to provide a safer, healthier environment. Through classes, career preparation training, and school and community organizations, there are numerous cocurricular opportunities for students to make a difference.

In one-on-one tutoring, older students help younger students to improve essential skills such as reading comprehension or math ability.

3

Helping Others Achieve

People achieve in many ways. Whether the goal is improving reading or math skills, understanding other cultures better, using technology, or winning competitions, there are many cocurricular service opportunities for students to help others succeed.

Mentoring takes a number of forms. Tutoring involves a short or long term experience with one person helping another. A high school student could teach a younger student reading or math skills or an older person computer skills. In peer tutoring, students may help their peers as a classroom aid or after school.

A mentor may be assigned to go to an elementary class for one period a day to meet a graduation requirement or earn service-learning credit; work within a classroom under the direction of the teacher to help one or a few students in that subject; or go to a retirement center or other facility for the elderly either during the school day, after school, or on weekends. Mentoring can even be accomplished via computer communications. Students at Florida Atlantic University serve as mentors to students in kindergarten through twelfth grade in an on-line literacy mentoring experience.

In Maryland, the Frederick County Service Learning Advisory Board, composed of area secondary school students, formed a partnership with an after-school program for at-risk youth. The advisory board students gave younger students homework support, served as positive role models, and worked with the students on combined service projects, such as an environmental garden project. As a result, the younger students not only improved in their schoolwork, they learned that it is important to help their community. The older students learned to plan projects, write grants, and mentor others.

Teens in Monterey, California, serve as Homework Pals through the public library. They volunteer to work with students from kindergarten to fifth grade for at least two hours a week after school. Many communities have homework and mentoring programs for young students through neighborhood service centers, elementary schools, and churches. These programs provide numerous opportunities for middle and high school students to get involved.

In a school-based mentoring activity, students from the Lincoln East DECA chapter in Nebraska participated in the local zoo's "Roaring for Reading" program. Chapter members read *Is Your Mama a Llama?* and five other books to elementary school students in support of the local education association's Harvest of Books Drive, which tries to give local first and second graders at least one new book.

Literacy service projects can cover many subjects. High school students in Easton, Maryland, present scenes from Shakespeare's plays to elementary students to familiarize

Peer tutoring matches students with members of their own class who may be having trouble with a particular subject. This type of tutoring can take place during free periods, study halls, or after school.

them with the famous playwright. Chemistry students present simple experiments to younger students. Advanced Spanish students develop learning activities for kindergarten students to introduce them to the language, then go to the elementary schools and present the information.

A Philadelphia math class wrote and designed books for children that included mathematical concepts. To prepare for the assignment, students read children's books, met with a children's book author, and discussed what makes a good children's book. After planning, writing, and illustrating their books, the students read them to local elementary school students and helped create a display of the books at the community library.

Students around the country use the concept of creating books to help others learn. Foreign language students create English vocabulary books for both elementary school students and community members who are learning English as a second language. These students also benefit as they increase their Spanish vocabulary and learn about other cultures. Other projects include creating simple alphabet books for entering preschoolers, then accompanying them on their first days of school and reading the alphabet book to them.

The "Sock It To Me Reading" project at Old Colony Regional Vocational Technical High School in Massachusetts won its National Honor Society (NHS) members national recognition and an NHS 2003 Outstanding Service Project Award. Members asked for donations of children's books, then each chose one of the books and created a sock puppet to use when reading the book to children. The books and puppets, along with the additional boxes of books, were then donated to area schools and preschools.

Homeless Children Like to Read, Too

Children in homeless shelters enjoy books as much as other children but may not have as much access to them. Students can tutor and read stories to children in homeless shelters. Students in North Carolina taped stories for children to be played on recorders that were donated to the shelters, according to the Kids Helping Kids Web site, **<www.kidshelpingkids.org>**. Michigan school and church youth groups worked together to collect school supplies, backpacks, and new and used books for shelter residents, along with winter hats and gloves. Two Massachusetts high school students opened a library in the basement of a homeless shelter through book drives, fundraisers, and grant writing. They said, "We believe that we have the potential to effect positive change for the poorest of the poor." They also hope that their efforts will help reduce homelessness.

School supplies make learning easier, but some children have very few of them. The Department of Social Services, churches, and area schools can serve as contacts for a local school supply project. Estimation contests (how many jelly beans in a jar, for example), book fairs, or penny drives are among the ways to raise funds for school supplies. Language arts skills come into play when students write to local organizations or businesses to tell them about their project and ask for their support.

The National Honor Society members in Hillsboro, Missouri, play Santa as they answer the letters written by kindergarten, first, and second grade students at a neighboring elementary school. Each member is given a class's letters to answer. Then the students dress as Santa's helpers and deliver the replies, giving each child a candy cane and helping them read Santa's letter.

In Maryland, the Montgomery County Ultimate Story Exchange (MUSE) is a partnership between an elementary school and members of the Communication Arts program at a nearby high school. Elementary students e-mail pieces of creative writing to their high school mentors, who offer suggestions, critiques, and compliments. The younger students benefit from the interaction with caring older students and the high school students serve as role models for their elementary correspondents.

While projects focusing on literacy and learning often involve younger students, there are service opportunities with all age levels. Senior citizens and those with disabilities are often in need of help due to health issues. Students can read to elderly persons or someone who has impaired sight. They can also make a class project of reading books or magazine articles on tape. Writing letters from dictation or helping someone figure out a shopping list and the cost of items are additional tasks student volunteers may perform.

Students from Dr. Nathan A. Pitts Elementary-Middle School in Baltimore, Maryland, were trained as mentors, tutors, and docents at the Port Discovery Kid-Powered Museum. Students were trained to help make visits to the museum more meaningful for younger children by assisting them with the interactive exhibits. Students had to complete a written application, be interviewed, and attend training sessions. Some students volunteered up to three hundred and fifty hours as junior guides, library assistants, exhibit monitors, and greeters.

Another way to serve the community is shown by Wakulla High School in Florida, where eleventh and twelfth graders in Technology Studies III were trained in computer repair and customer service. Afterwards, they carried out repair and training projects in the community, including service for the public library and the county commissioners. In Philadelphia, the Urban Technology Project "challenges students to become technology leaders in their community." After conducting a survey to determine the community's technology needs, students established a center for recycling and refurbishing computers. Students also receive technology and computer repair training to become "Tech Teens" who offer technical support to places that received the computers.

Older citizens enjoy learning about computers, too. Members of Lions-Quest, a community service group at Evergreen Park High School in Illinois, present a six-week course to their senior citizen partners. Meeting once a week, the pairs tackle subjects such as word processing and e-mail, surfing the Internet, and playing computer games.

Service projects can also help community members

Members of Y-Art, a collective that provides artistic opportunities to young people in Santa Cruz, California, work with community members on a mural for the Beach Flats neighborhood.

understand one another better and appreciate diversity. At the Academy for Science and Foreign Language in Huntsville, Alabama, students researched African-American history and culture and documented the contributions of African Americans to Huntsville. After using communication skills to conduct interviews and math and science skills to determine and analyze environmental changes, students incorporated this information in stories and created accompanying computer-generated lesson plans and multimedia kits. The project resulted in a greater community-wide respect for, and understanding and appreciation of, cultural differences and contributions.

Some Maryland ninth grade English classes learned about tolerance through literature selections addressing poverty, prejudice, war, and disabilities. After reading, discussion, and additional preparation, the freshmen teamed up with students from an area school for students with severe physical and mental challenges. A joint service project, field trips, and recreational activities provided the freshmen with the opportunity to be mentors as they interacted with their partners.

Student council members at Pennridge High School in Pennsylvania partner with a facility for special needs adults to provide a prom for them in the school cafeteria. Music, refreshments, and dance partners from the student council are event features. According to their advisor, the students enjoy hosting the event as much as their guests enjoy attending it.

An athletic peer mentoring experience can be achieved

Promoting Literacy Abroad

Children who experience disasters both natural (droughts, floods) and manmade (military or political conflicts) often find their lives in upheaval. Their homes might be damaged or destroyed, their belongings gone, their schools looted or closed.

The Red Cross School Chest project **<www.redcross.org>** gives students the opportunity to let other children have what most take for granted—school supplies to help them with their education. Classes that participate in the School Chest project receive information on the recipient country, ideas for class activities, and a list of the required objects, enough to supply a class of forty students. Sometimes class members bring in materials; other times they hold bake sales, flower sales, or other fundraisers in order to purchase them.

Recent countries receiving school chests include El Salvador, Kenya, Afghanistan, and the Dominican Republic.

through participation in the Special Olympics programs held nationwide. This international organization empowers students who have a variety of disabilities "to become physically fit, productive and respected members of society through sports training and competition." North Penn High School in Pennsylvania hosted the Montgomery County Region Spring Track and Field Special Olympics. National Honor Society members planned and organized the entire event, including curriculum development and training sessions for volunteers. Almost one-third of the student body volunteered and participated in the Special Olympics track meet. Every competing athlete received a ribbon for participating. As a result of these efforts, the North Penn High School National Honor Society Chapter was recognized as School of the Year by the Pennsylvania Special Olympics Organization and their project was hailed as one of the ten outstanding service projects recognized by the National Honor Society that year.

Whether helping with school subjects, creating reading opportunities, gathering school supplies, helping with technology, or assisting others to excel physically, cocurricular community service projects result in rewarding feelings for all involved.

The Plant a Row for the Hungry campaign encourages farmers and gardeners to donate surplus produce to local food banks, soup kitchens, and service agencies to help feed America's hungry.

4

Serving to Provide Basic Needs

Homelessness, hunger, poverty, companionship—these are all examples of areas in which students can serve to help others meet their basic needs. Community service is about meeting these needs and much more.

One chapter of Future Business Leaders of America (FBLA) chose to perform a variety of projects for nursing home residents for Make A Difference Day, a national service event. The students planted flowers, helped at mealtime, and attended church services with the residents. They also made and delivered treat bags. In these ways, the FBLA members showed the older citizens that they were not alone or ignored.

Students from Howard High School in Delaware spent their Make A Difference Day at an area apartment building, providing manicures (cosmetology students), informing residents of free dental products (dental assisting students), and taking blood pressure and heartbeat readings (nursing students) while other students ran games and taught

Ismael Caballero, a sixteen-year-old Habitat for Humanity volunteer from Aleman Santamaria High School, volunteers at a home building project in Cochabama, Bolivia, in 2001.

computer skills to the residents, many of whom had graduated from the same high school years earlier.

Technology Student Association (TSA) middle school members in Virginia Beach, Virginia, made pre-Christmas visits to residents of the local healthcare and rehabilitation center. The students met after school to make decorations, creating over two hundred ornaments in three weeks. Though they were nervous when they first walked in, the warm welcome the TSA members received quickly made them comfortable as they chatted with the residents. The center's therapeutic recreation director said, "Most people think about children during the holidays, but there are adults here, too, in need of love." A resident added, "It's wonderful when a child thinks about people in the hospital, especially the elderly." By the end of the visit, the students knew that the residents had really appreciated their efforts.

Health Occupations Students of America (HOSA) members sponsor an evening where chapter members meet to socialize, snack, and make gifts for the elderly. The HOSA members then deliver the gifts to local nursing homes and provide some holiday cheer.

Middle school students in Queen Anne's County, Maryland, read selections involving elderly characters, practiced their communication skills, received sensitivity training, and had presentations by guest speakers to prepare for their service experience. They wrote letters to local seniors, made them holiday cards, interviewed them, held a party for them, and had a joint picnic. The students' project ended with a photo album of their activities that they could share with school and community members.

Recognizing that older people enjoy parties too, Kaitlyn Sutherland, a Service Learning Advisory Board student in Frederick County, Maryland, created a project called "Stars and Stripes Senior-Senior Prom." She and her fellow advisory board members arranged with the horticulture class for corsages, prepared the refreshments and decorations, and met with the staff of the nearby senior daycare center to plan and finalize arrangements. At the event, the dancing, socializing, and refreshments resulted in a positive intergenerational experience for students and seniors.

In the same vein, student council members at Phoenix High School in New York hold a yearly senior citizens' ball that includes dressing up, a buffet, and even group wheelchair dancing. Student council president Stacey Cook said, "Every year our students are deeply touched by the connection made with these very special people." She concluded by saying that the senior citizens are just as touched because these students took time out of their busy lives for the seniors.

Service activities result in learning. A class of eighth graders in Philadelphia paired with senior citizens at local retirement centers for their "Generations" project. First, students learned about nursing homes and retirement centers. Then they learned how to communicate with the residents and found out that they might need to talk loudly and clearly or type written material in large font. During their meetings with their senior citizen partners, students shared information about their likes and dislikes, interviewed their partners, and shared interests and hobbies. Some of the students and senior citizens exchanged holiday cards or showed family photographs. Their final product, copies of the oral histories they had written based on their interviews, were shared at a celebration attended by many of the senior citizens. For some students, this experience also resulted in new job and career choices.

Another issue facing some people is a lack of food or appropriate clothing. Toys are also scarce. To do their part in remedying this situation, the DECA chapter at North Gwinnett High School in Georgia made a Toys for Tots campaign their largest service project ever, gathering over two thousand toys as a result of their appeals to students, businesses, and community associations.

A clothing drive for Baltimore City foster children was conducted by seventh-grade students from a neighboring county. Students wrote to local businesses for donations of clothing or money, performed in skits on the school's in-house television network, created a Web page for their project, and managed the daily collecting, sorting, and storing of the clothing. At the end of the project, over 6,000 pieces of clothing, 178 pairs of shoes, and $400 for purchasing underwear had been collected and presented to the Baltimore Department of Social Services.

In Columbia, South Carolina, high school Spanish language students developed a project to serve the growing Hispanic population. Thanks to their efforts, more than twenty tons of food, clothing, household products, and medicine were collected and distributed.

A clothing drive called "Stuff-A-Bus" was jointly held by the seven schools in Caroline County, Maryland. The project resulted in a school bus loaded with 7,920 pounds of food and clothing for a local food and clothing pantry and women's shelter. Collection projects in other parts of the nation include gathering suitcases for foster children, who often have few belongings and no way to carry them.

Working Together for Home Improvement

Many people want to remain independently living in their homes as long as they possibly can. However, because of disabilities, low income, or other factors, some citizens cannot keep their houses in the best condition or make needed repairs.

Rebuilding Together **<www.rebuildingtogether.org>**, the nation's largest volunteer housing rehabilitation organization, is the only national organization that focuses solely on the home repair and improvement needs of lower-income homeowners. Originally known as Christmas in April, the name was changed in 2000 to acknowledge that people needed these services at all times of the year, not just in April.

For over ten years, career and technology students, along with students in other classes and organizations, have joined together in Frederick County, Maryland, to repair more than twenty homes each year. By doing so, they better understand the differences of living standards in their own county and realize that they can make a positive difference in someone's life.

Becky Sutter and Jamie Smith, student volunteers, work on the framing of a Habitat for Humanity house in Columbus, Georgia, in 2003.

While some people may not think of glasses as clothing, they are essential items for those whose sight is impaired. DECA members at Florida's Chamberlain High School collected used prescription eyeglasses in their school and community. The finale of the project was when they teamed with the Florida Aquarium, collecting used children's eyeglasses in place of the price of admission. They were also on hand to provide face-painting and sea-costumed characters. The eyeglasses from this project were donated to children in Honduras.

Going to a job interview without being appropriately dressed is a poor first impression to give a prospective employer. The National Honor Society at Northern Highlands Regional High School in New Jersey conducted a clothing drive for adults on welfare who were seeking a job but did not have the proper clothing to interview or work in an office setting. Business suits, blouses, skirts, shirts, and jackets were among the items collected and donated for distribution. NHS members at Booker T. Washington High School in Oklahoma collected donations of new underwear and socks and donated these to a local day center for the homeless. Clients can shower, eat, and receive new underclothes and hygiene items when they come to the center.

Another project involving clothing and food is conducted by the Student Council at Georgia's Duluth High School. Understanding that some seniors may not be able to attend their prom because of the expense involved in appropriate dress and dining costs, they ask for donations of dresses and tuxedos for four senior boys and four senior girls. Additionally, they ask area merchants to donate the dinners and the cost of the tickets. The items are then presented to the seniors confidentially by school administrators so that not even the student council members who worked on the project know who received the items.

Nutritious food is not always easily available to persons in need, so many schools and organizations conduct food drives. For several years the DECA chapter at Southeast Raleigh High School in North Carolina has collected canned goods on a special day at the State Fair. A donation of at least four cans per person takes the place of admission fees. The National Guard had to use its trucks to transport all the donated cans to the North Carolina Food Bank.

In Washington state, West Valley High School National Honor Society members put a different twist on the standard food drive. Members took turns standing outside area grocery stores, handing out fliers that asked for donations of baby food, a relatively inexpensive item, for a local food bank. They found that the people they interacted with responded well to their request.

Instead of trick-or-treating, members of Kansas's Trego High School Family, Consumer and Community Leaders of America (FCCLA) dressed up in costumes and went door to door collecting canned goods for the local Red Cross chapter. They had advertised their project beforehand so that community members would be ready to contribute.

Members of the agricultural education organization FFA have participated in WAGN, the Washington Area Gleaning Network. Along with many other volunteers, FFA members help to collect, sort, and send to food banks millions of pounds of fresh fruits and vegetables that would otherwise be left lying in the fields because of imperfections in color or shape. The Plant a Row for the Hungry campaign encourages students and their families to work together to grow vegetables for the food bank, as students at Maryland's Hereford Middle School did. They even had a display at the Maryland Home and Flower Show to tell the public about their project.

"Making Service and Service-Learning the Common Expectation and Common Experience of All Young People in America" is a goal of Youth Service America. In 2003, this organization joined with America's All Stars, the Salvation Army, and Campbell Soup to host the "world's largest Thanksgiving dinner." Students organized fund-raising dinners at their own schools. Then the money and donated items were sent to local branches of the Salvation Army nationwide to help people in need. "As our greatest asset, it is only fitting that young people play a lead role in meeting community needs, while lending their time, ener-gy, commitment, and experience," said Steve Culbertson, president and CEO of Youth Service America. The project

Jessie Abbott and Marta Holstad, student volunteers from Franklin High School in Seattle, Washington, volunteer for Habitat for Humanity in Cochabama, Bolivia, in 2001.

gave students a hands-on opportunity to help those in need and served as a character development event.

The "Empty Bowls" project both raises awareness and funds for those in need. The project begins when students make clay bowls in or after school. Florida's South Lake High School involves about two hundred students in a wide variety of areas, such as digital design, culinary arts, and fine arts. The older students use the technology presentations that they designed to inform elementary students about poverty and the Empty Bowls project, then teach the students to make clay bowls. The bowls are sold at the Empty Bowls "dinner" and the funds raised are given to nonprofit organizations that help families in need.

A place to live is a basic need. Some people have no home, while others have homes that are in disrepair. As a homelessness awareness and fundraiser project, FCCLA members from Pomperaugh High School in Connecticut collect pledges to spend the night in large cardboard boxes that act as their "homeless shelter." If it rains, they are allowed to bring tarps, but the event goes on regardless of the weather. Several district student councils in Texas ask for donations of materials to weatherize homes for low income residents in their area, and they make improvements to about twenty houses a year.

Habitat for Humanity has chapters both nationally and internationally to eliminate poverty housing from the world. Many schools have student Habitat chapters. The Habitat for Humanity Web site has a variety of suggestions for ways in which students can help. Elementary students can make a welcome basket for the new homeowners, stock their pantry, or make house-shaped banks for fundraising. Middle level students can landscape the yard,

"Feel Better" Blankets

Project Linus, a volunteer nonprofit organization, provides new, homemade, washable blankets and afghans to children who are very ill, traumatized, or otherwise in need. The idea for Project Linus came as a result of a 1995 magazine interview in which a child stated that her security blanket helped her get through her chemotherapy sessions. Reader Karen Loucks decided to provide homemade blankets to an area children's cancer center. As word of her efforts spread, the project grew nationwide. For example, sewing events sponsored by a Maryland Project Linus Club resulted in over three hundred fifty blankets.

The Project Linus Web site gives information on patterns and sizes for quilts, afghans, or blankets. For more information, contact **<www.projectlinus.org>**.

plant window boxes for the new home or sell them as fundraisers, design a T-shirt to be sold at a Habitat event, or paint doors and baseboards away from the construction site. Students ages sixteen and older can build picnic tables for the work site, tutor younger partner family children, or get the finished house ready for the dedication.

Technology Student Association members from Windham Middle and High Schools in Connecticut build a playhouse that is then donated to the local chapter of Habitat for Humanity to be raffled as a fundraiser. The playhouse project, which has been going on for over ten years, usually raises $600 to $800 a year. The nearly 400-member Habitat chapter at Pope High School in Georgia raised about $10,000 at a prom fashion show and silent auction.

There are many other ways to help meet people's needs. Some students collect supplies for troops overseas or send letters to servicemen and women. Others raise money for children with special needs to attend camps, or collect teddy bears for police personnel to give to children who are scared or upset.

There are many needs in the world. Community service projects help to make a difference in people's lives, enriching both the students and the recipients.

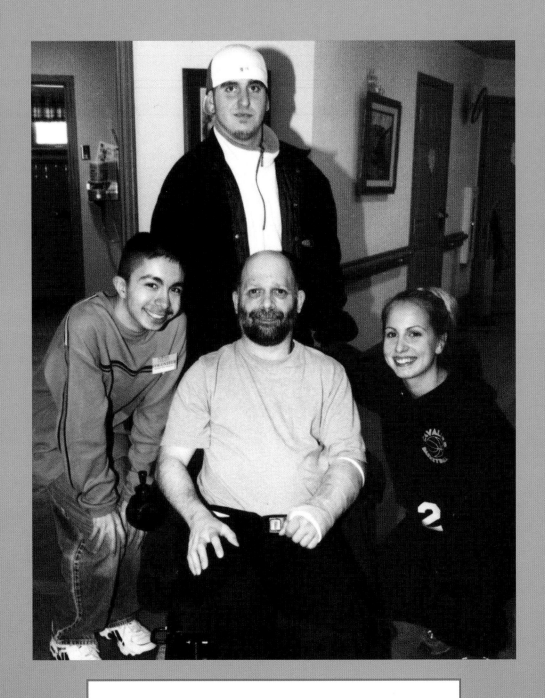

As part of their senior project, students from Thomas More High School in St. Francis, Wisconsin, volunteer their time at a local day care program for disabled adults.

5

Caring for the Community

There are many cocurricular service projects that deal with environmental issues. Students in four Philadelphia middle schools built embankments for turtles and worked on a bridge that crosses plains flooded by a hurricane. Eighth graders in another urban school investigated pollution control and produced educational materials for both children and adults. Students at Coral Springs High School in Florida developed environmental storybooks and audiotapes for elementary students to use to improve reading skills. Students in Syracuse, New York, worked to establish a city flower and vegetable garden.

Other community environmental projects include planting submerged aquatic grasses, renovating areas for erosion control, and restoring and monitoring local streams. The preservation of historic cemeteries combines environmental and social studies elements as students care for the land and research original documentation of the cemeteries and the persons buried there.

Wildlife is also a community service focus. White River High School students in Washington used DNA fingerprinting and calculator-based laboratory procedures to bring the Chinook King Salmon back from near extinction. In Monterey, California, students sixteen or older can join the Sea Lion Watch, discouraging sea lions from staying near docks for both human and sea lion safety. Other groups build duck and bat boxes to increase habitat options.

Projects centering on veterans help the community to remember the past and recognize the challenges that fellow community members once faced. Some student groups host Veterans' Day breakfasts and assemblies. Others carry out activities such as sending flowers, posters, cookies, cards, or letters to veterans' hospitals or organizations. Some groups have compiled oral histories by interviewing area veterans. This information is then combined with student research of events at that time in history to produce a more complete account of local veterans' experiences.

There are many community organizations with youth branches. Civitan International's Junior Civitan clubs are a community service organization for young people. Some of these clubs focus on environmental education of the public, while others adopt a highway, stream, or acre of rainforest. They may help build a community playground or conduct fundraisers for charities.

EXCEL Clubs, sponsored by Exchange Clubs, are groups of high school members who serve their communities in many ways, such as bicycle safety programs, "Breakfast with Santa" programs, youth mentoring, or Read Across America Day activities.

Key Clubs and Builders Clubs are both sponsored by Kiwanis International. Middle school students in the Builders Club can organize food and clothing drives, raise

A student volunteer for the Pritzker-Cousins Youth Build works on the framing of a Habitat for Humanity house in Robbins, Tennessee.

money for playground or computer equipment, or adopt a resident at a senior citizens facility as some of their activities. High school students in the Key Club participate in "Seasons of Service" projects: March of Dimes, Read and Lead, UNICEF, and Children's Miracle Network, along with individual club projects.

Rotary International's Interact Club is open to students fourteen to eighteen. Interact members participate in at least two community service projects each year, including one which promotes international understanding and goodwill. The Easton, Maryland, High School Interact Club sponsored a young girl in Africa and received letters from her, which members answered. Interact Clubs exist in over one hundred countries.

Lions Clubs International not only sponsors Leo Clubs for members twelve to twenty-eight, they also sponsor school-based groups, Scout troops, and other local youth groups. As do many of the community groups already mentioned, Lions Clubs International sponsors awards to recognize students for their service to their communities as they follow the organization's motto, "We serve." Young people participate in projects in service areas such as recreation, health issues, safety, and the environment.

Members of the Boy Scouts, Girl Scouts, and Camp Fire

Tips on Volunteering

The President's Volunteer Service Award recognizes all students from kindergarten through college who contribute at least one hundred hours to the community. These students receive a gold lapel pin, a certificate, and a letter from the president. Students from five to fourteen can receive a silver lapel pin, certificate, and letter for completing at least fifty hours of service. In addition, middle and high schools nationwide are recognized for their excellence in service-learning and are honored as National Service-Learning Leader Schools.

The Web site <www.presidentialserviceawards.org> includes these tips on volunteering:

- Research the issues important to you.

- Think about the skills you have.

- Decide if you would like a new skill or experience to be part of the service.

- Look for a service project that goes along with other goals you already have.

- Make sure you have enough time to do the task well.

You may want to consider a community service project you can do alone, with friends, or with family members. As you participate, keep your sense of humor and realize that when you give of yourself to others you gain a lot in personal accomplishment and satisfaction.

USA are busy with service projects, too. Boy Scout Troop 2000 in Colorado has improved and maintained an area trail. Girl Scouts from the Mile Hi Council in Colorado collect food, clothing, personal hygiene items, and toys for later redistribution to low-resource families. They have also made blankets for preschool children, collected new and slightly used teddy bears to be given to children in crisis, and cleaned and planted garden beds. Camp Fire USA teens choose a national topic as the focus of their National Youth Campaign service projects for a two-year period. Some recent topics have been global awareness and hunger and homelessness.

Elks Lodges sponsor Scout troops, Boys and Girls Clubs, 4-H programs, other youth organizations, and youth athletics and arts programs. In May, Elks National Youth Week recognizes young people for their contributions to their community and their achievements.

Moose International sponsors a youth awareness program. At Moose Association Student Congresses, over fourteen hundred teens come together to discuss issues of importance in their communities and strategies to address these issues. Participants create presentations for younger children. High school students also speak with preschool and elementary students about topics that promote positive lifestyles.

Service to the community does not go unrecognized. Almost all community organizations recognize youth volunteers for their efforts, as do schools and local governments. The Prudential Spirit of Community Awards and the President's Volunteer Service Awards are examples of community service recognitions. Make A Difference Day, held on the last Saturday in October each year, provides recognition in *USA Weekend Magazine* articles and $10,000

Helping out older adults with their lawn work is a great idea for a community service project. Students can rake leaves, remove brush, or do whatever is needed by the homeowner.

grants given to ten recipients to continue their projects. These awards, totaling $100,000, are given by actor Paul Newman from the profits of his food product line, Newman's Own. All of the Newman's Own company profits are donated to educational and charitable organizations.

On the Lions-Quest Web site, a student expressed her service experiences by saying, "I think service should be a part of education. You can't learn everything you know from a textbook. You learn from other people."

"Before [service class] I thought that I wasn't qualified or old enough to help," said another student. "Now I realize that it's everyone's responsibility . . . In my opinion once you start with service, you won't stop."

As more students become involved in cocurricular and community-based service projects, they understand better the relationships between themselves, their community, their peers, their real-world application of what they have learned, and their role in the future of their community and world.

Glossary

endow–to furnish with funds to support.

facilitator–a person who makes a discussion or process easier.

foundation–an institution with funds given for its permanent support.

grant–a gift, often money, to be used for a particular purpose.

initiative–an introductory step.

internship–a program in which students receive supervised practical experience.

literacy–the ability to read and write.

mediation–to work with opposing sides to settle a dispute.

mentor–tutor, coach, or counselor.

mobilize–to put into movement.

refurbish–to brighten or freshen up.

resolution–a statement expressing the opinion, will, or intent of a group.

rehabilitate–to restore to good condition or health.

service-learning–a teaching method that combines meaningful service to the community with a curricular learning component.

therapeutic–relating to or dealing with healing.

tolerance–allowing for beliefs or practices differing from one's own.

traumatize–to cause mental or physical injury, usually by an outside agent.

weatherize–to make something better protected against winter weather.

Internet Resources

www.learningindeed.org
Learning In Deed promotes national service-learning.

www.pointsoflight.org
Offers information on mobilizing people and resources for community needs.

www.habitat.org
The Habitat for Humanity Web site includes project suggestions for ages five and up.

www.redcross.org
Includes information on the Red Cross school chest project.

www.youthgrantmakers.org
Web site for the Youth Advisory Committees.

www.presidentialserviceawards.org
Information on the awards and recent recipients.

www.humaneteen.org
Information on the Humane Teen of the Year honorees.

www.nhs.org
Information on outstanding service projects recognized by the National Honor Society.

www.lions-quest.org
The youth service initiative of Lions Clubs International.

www.nationalhomeless.org
Provides examples of ways young people can help the homeless.

www.ysa.org
Information on National Youth Service Day and Global Youth Service Day.

Further Reading

Emmer, Rae. *Community Service.* New York: Power Kids Press, 2002.

Kielburger, Marc and Craig. *Take Action! A Guide to Active Citizenship.* New York: John Wiley & Sons, 2002.

Lewis, Barbara, and Pamela Espeland. *The Kid's Guide to Service Projects: Over 500 Service Ideas for Young People Who Want to Make A Difference.* Minneapolis, Minnesota: Free Spirit Publishing, 1995.

Rusch, Elizabeth. *Generation Fix: Young Ideas for a Better World.* Hillsboro, Oregon: Beyond Words Publishing, 2002.

Ryan, Bernard. *Expanding Education and Literacy* (Community Service for Teens series). New York: Ferguson Publishing, 1998.

Index

PICTURE CREDITS

Cover: Benjamin Stewart, PhotoDisc.
Interior: P.R. News Foto/Tyson Foods: 2; Photos.com: 8, 40; Courtesy of E. Crittendon at Taos Community Fund: 10; P.R. News Foto/Boys & Girls Club of America: 13; P.R. News Foto/North County Humane Society: 14; P.R. News Foto/Olive Garden: 16; Courtesy of www.JoinHandsDay.org: 19; Courtesy of FCCLA: 24; Courtesy of the National Student Campaign Against Hunger and Homelessness: 28, Lisa Hochstein: 37; ©Oscar C. Williams: 30, 33; Denise Muschel/Habitat for Humanity International: 42; Steffan Hacker/ Habitat for Humanity International: 46; Kim MacDonald/ Habitat for Humanity International: 49; ©Ron Walloch Photography: 52; Robert Baker/Habitat for Humanity International: 55; ©Ulrich Tutsch: 58.

ABOUT THE AUTHOR

Terry Callahan teaches at Easton High School in Maryland. She is a Service-Learning Fellow through the Maryland State Department of Education Youth Development Division.

SERIES CONSULTANT

Series Consultant Sharon L. Ransom is Chief Officer of the Office of Standards-Based Instruction for Chicago Public Schools and Lecturer at the University of Illinois at Chicago. She is the founding director of the Achieving High Standards Project: a Standards-Based Comprehensive School Reform project at the University of Illinois at Chicago, and she is the former director of the Partnership READ Project: a Standards Based Change Process. Her work has included school reform issues that center on literacy instruction, as well as developing standards-based curriculum and assessments, improving school leadership, and promoting school, parent, and community partnerships. In 1999, she received the Martin Luther King Outstanding Educator's Award.